6 Report

After Grenfell: the Faith Groups' Response

Amy Plender

Foreword by by Elizabeth Oldfield

After Grenfell: the Faith Groups' Response

"Combining thorough research and incisive analysis, *After Grenfell* is an indispensable guide to the faith groups of North Kensington, and their response to the Grenfell fire. A range of witnesses testify to the lively presence of faith in the community, and offer invaluable insights into qualities of engagement and service that began long before the disaster, and will continue into the future. Amy Plender's compassionate and attentive listening is a model for us all, as together we seek to build the City of God in our midst."

Revd Prebendary Dr Alan Everett, vicar of St Clement and St James, in whose parish Grenfell Tower stands

"This report is a very useful reflection of the events that followed the tragic fire at Grenfell Tower on 14 June 2017. We at Al-Manaar believe that documenting the tragedy and its aftermath is important and will assist in any future review and evaluation exercises."

Abdurahman Sayed, CEO of Al-Manaar Muslim Cultural Heritage Centre, near Grenfell Tower

After Grenfell: the Faith Groups' Response

"This is a welcome report and I hope it will stand as a timely insight for the future. I witnessed the fire at Grenfell Tower with my daughter who was 10 years old at the time. As the fire grew worse I could only turn to my Heavenly Father and pray. Many of us prayed that night. It was 5.15am in the morning when young Muslim men brought water as they were on their way to the mosque during Ramadan; it was the nearby churches that opened their doors to give shelter and accept the large number of donations pouring in; it was the gurdwara that set up the first hot food operation under the Westway. The Justice 4 Grenfell campaign was launched on five days later on 19 June with a silent walk. The walk is led by survivors, bereaved families and leaders of all faiths. The community has leant on many local faith leaders for strength and support following the disaster. Working in a multi-faith way has enabled us to have a deeper dialogue about our faith. It will, I pray, also change the discourse of the importance of faith in North Kensington. The Grenfell disaster has made our community stronger and for many our faith is much deeper. All faith groups should recognise the fantastic response they gave to the fire. They should also recognise and go forward with the aim of continuing to work in a multi faith way as the standard practice in our community. Grenfell is the proof that they can do this, God willing."

Yvette Williams, MBE, Justice 4 Grenfell, Campaign Co-ordinator

Contents

Contents

Acknowledgements	7
Foreword – Elizabeth Oldfield	8
Introduction	12
1 What the faith groups did	19
2 How they were able to do it	43
3 Lessons from Grenfell	52
Conclusion	73
Appendices	81

Acknowledgements

Acknowledgements

This report would not have been possible without the support of its participants. Our interviewees and others who contributed to the research gave up their time and welcomed the author into their workplaces and homes, to tell us about what had often been a deeply painful and traumatic experience. Their generosity, wisdom, and dignity in sharing these experiences with us, along with the professional insights of civic, emergency, and charity personnel, cannot be understated. This report is directly based on the voices of our participants – though it should go without saying that any errors are the responsibility of the author.

Amy Plender,
London, May 2018

Foreword – Elizabeth Oldfield

Foreword – Elizabeth Oldfield

The fire at Grenfell Tower, on 14 June 2017 shocked and horrified the country, the agony and trauma of its victims compounded by the apparent indifference and disorganization that ensued.

In the chaos, the role of the diverse faith groups in the community stood out. Churches, mosques, synagogues, and gurdwaras all stepped up to the plate, responding practically, emotionally and spiritually to a moment of pain and confusion. This report explores what they did, how they managed to do it, and what can be learned from the experience.

It is important to be clear, at the outset, about what this report is not. It is not a study of how the fire started, or who was responsible, or why the Council response was felt by so many to be so inadequate. Nor is it an attempt to claim that the faith groups' response was flawless – as more than one interviewee commented, there could be no such thing as a flawless response to such a tragedy – or that no other community group did or could response to the disaster. Rather, it is simply and narrowly a study into how the faith groups did respond and what can be learned from it.

Amy Plender interviewed over thirty people in the community, from faith groups, statutory groups, emergency services, and beyond, who were involved in responding to the tragedy. She asked them what they did, what they would have done differently and what the experience taught them about the role of faith in contemporary Britain. The responses were instructive – moving, challenging, inspiring, and honest – and kept on returning to a number of key themes.

The faith groups were able to respond in the way they did because they were *trusted*. They were *embedded in the communities* they served. Indeed, they were made up of people from the local community itself. In many ways, the faith response was an example of the community ministering to itself, rather than being helped by well-meaning outsiders.

In addition, the faith groups had a history, they were *long-standing institutions*, having been in existence there for a long time, their presence in the community not temporary or contingent on immediate funding, but steadfast. They were in it for the long haul.

Finally, the faith groups were *committed*. Community is a popular word today, and with popularity has come vagueness: people who share almost anything are considered a community. In contrast, these faith groups were committed, dedicated to both their faith and their community. This resulted in a valuable combination: of having invested sufficiently in their localities to the effect that they owned and ran buildings and facilities and also of preaching and practicing an ethos of openness and hospitality to those in need, which meant they could open those buildings and use those facilities for those who needed them.

As a result, they were able to respond to the needs of the moment: not perfectly perhaps – as noted, there is no such thing as a 'perfect' response to such an event – but rapidly, compassionately and holistically.

The experience taught them – and can teach us – many things, lessons worth heeding for any future response. Three are worth highlighting.

First, *be prepared*. We hope nothing like Grenfell will ever happen again, but even if it does not, no community is immune from the potential for tragedy, whether it be terrorism, flooding, or the kind of knife crime that is currently plaguing

London. Being 'prepared' for these events – in the sense of building good networks, communications and relationships with statutory and other civil society bodies, establishing databases of potential volunteers, and even practicing emergency responses – might make all the difference.

Second, *be visible*. We repeatedly heard that, in the chaos of the immediate aftermath, being identifiable as coming from a trusted faith group made a difference. The same lesson applies elsewhere. Being at a tragedy is important, but being visible there can be even more so, as it shows how society is not made up simply of innumerable, anonymous individuals, but rather people with affiliations and associations, on which they can draw in times of need.

Finally, *be flexible*. When it came to offers of practical help, of financial assistance, or pastoral care, it really helps to understand and respond to the context. Being embedded in a community, knowing a locality, and having networks can enable the kind of flexible response that a disaster like Grenfell demands. Faith groups are well positioned here but need to think creatively about their flexibility, as any other group would.

Grenfell was a horrendous tragedy, which ended over 70 lives, damaged hundreds more, and shocked millions. Yet, while it revealed signs of vulnerability, inequality and even indifference, it also showed a community that could respond with real courage and commitment. Much of that response was seen in the faith groups' efforts. We hope that this report will raise the public profile of that work and offer valuable lessons for the future.

Elizabeth Oldfield
Director, Theos

Introduction

The Grenfell Tower fire was, in terms of lives lost, the worst fire since the Second World War.[1] Its repercussions were devastating for all those living in and around the Tower but reached far beyond the immediate neighbourhood. Some estimates place the number of those in some way directly affected at over 11,000, presenting the single largest mental-health challenge of its kind in Europe.[2] Moreover, the nature, reasons and response to the fire exposed social fissures and tensions that reverberated across the nation.

Grenfell Tower was built in the early 1970s as part of the regeneration of North Kensington.[3] Rising 24 storeys high, it had six flats on each floor, apart from the first few floors which were designated for office and community space.[4] About 600 people are believed to have been resident in June 2017.[5] The tower block dominates the North Kensington skyline, and concerns around its 'unsightliness,' as well as its energy efficiency, led the local council, The Royal Borough of Kensington and Chelsea (RBKC), to install cladding over it in 2015. This cladding would turn out to fail basic safety requirements, and at the time of writing, was deemed to be a main contributor to the scale of the fire on 14 June 2017.[6]

The scale of the Grenfell Tower fire was met only by the scale of the emergency and voluntary response. From the earliest hours, the news reports covered the involvement of the local residents and volunteers, including the local faith groups.[7] This report provides an overview of the faith groups' response to the tragedy and underlines how much was done by how many, in a way that was marked by deep local knowledge, networks, trust, pastoral sensitivity, and professionalism.

The faith groups were by no means the only groups to respond to the fire and its aftermath. Other groups present included the emergency services, statutory bodies, and other local voluntary organisations, in particular The Westway Sports and Fitness Centre, The Rugby Portobello Trust, and The Harrow Club, as well as national secular charities, such as The Red Cross and Citizens UK.

This report focusses primarily on the response of the faith groups for three main reasons. First, a number of reports at the time identified the role that faith groups played in response to the fire, and as a religion and society think tank, this was of particular interest to us at Theos. Second, given the sometimes hostile narrative that has grown up around 'faith' in certain circles today, the story of the faith groups' response needs to be better known. Third, although the evidence shows that the faith groups' response was overwhelmingly positive and well-received, there is no guarantee that churches or other faith groups would be able to react like that again, or could do so in other areas of the UK. Thus, one objective of this report is to glean some of the lessons accumulated by the Grenfell faith groups so that they can be more widely understood and shared, as a way of helping other groups respond to any subsequent tragedies.

In the research phase of the report, we first approached faith leaders based in the community around Grenfell. Having described the remit and intentions of our research, we then invited them to interview, on the understanding that these conversations would form the basis of our report (a full explanation of our ethics procedures and a sample interview guide, along with a list of our interviewees, can be found in the appendices at the back of this report). Interviews were held in private, at a location of the interviewee's choice, with just the researcher and interviewee present (although interviewees were invited to bring along a chaperone or support person if they wished to, none took this up). As the interviews developed, and we gained more understanding of the faith communities of North Kensington, we were made aware of more faith centres and leaders, usually through personal recommendation of the interviewees themselves. This organic approach allowed us the best possible insight into the local community, as it developed primarily through word of mouth from those living and working there.

The interview phase concluded, we were able to identify key themes arising from the collated results, which form the body of this report. An early draft of the report was distributed to the interviewees for clarification and fact-checking, and their feedback incorporated into the final draft.

This report proceeds as follows. First, we sketch the community of North Kensington (where Grenfell Tower stands), and the local faith groups. We then detail the faith groups' immediate responses, from (1) opening their doors in the early hours on 14 June, to (2) managing the practical resources of donations and volunteers, and (3) their pastoral response of offering prayer and emotional support in the very short term. We then look at (4) how this pastoral, psychological, and emotional support has continued, through the sixth-month anniversary service at St. Paul's Cathedral, to lesser known initiatives and programmes run by the faith groups in and for their local communities. Lastly, (5) we explore how the perceived failings of the Council and other bodies had an impact on the extent to which faith groups felt called upon to act.

In Part 2, we then analyse what contributed to the faith groups' ability to respond. In particular, our interviewees attributed this to one or more of three themes: (1) the trust the faith groups had established, through their longevity, being rooted in their communities, and through having relationship and communication networks; (2) the available space in their worship spaces, halls, and storage facilities, and (3) their ability to balance professionalism and established protocols with flexibility and reacting quickly to events as they unfolded.

In Part 3, we lay out what we heard from interviewees about what they had learnt in their responses to Grenfell which they felt would be useful for faith and community groups facing any future disasters. Broadly these fell into:

(1) preparation: for faith groups to develop and practise their emergency responses; to be confident about their ability to respond in a crisis; and to develop and strengthen networks and working relationships and friendships with other faith and civic groups in the community.

(2) visibility: the need to use uniform and/or other identity markers to ensure visibility, both for practical reasons of making oneself seen, but also as a means of establishing one's faith group as present in solidarity with a community in crisis; and lastly

(3) flexibility: to be adaptable, willing and able to identify which are the most pressing needs; to accept offers of help from those able to give it and decline help and donations when surplus to requirements; and to provide person-centred, religiously- and culturally-appropriate aid, not assuming all people affected by a crisis will have the same set of needs and being willing and able to accommodate those variables.

Overall, we hope that this report not only helps bring (further) recognition to the important and life-affirming work that faith groups did in the wake of an enormous human tragedy, but also that, in exploring *how* they were able to respond in the way they did, it offers lessons that might benefit us all.

[1] Nadifa Mohammad, 'Britain's hostile environment has been a century in the making', The Guardian, 29 April 2018. https://www.theguardian.com/commentisfree/2018/apr/29/britain-hostile-environment-century-making-migrants-brutality-windrush-scandal

[2] Press Association, 'Grenfell Tower mental health response "largest of its kind in Europe"', The Guardian, 30 October 2017. https://www.theguardian.com/uk-news/2017/oct/30/grenfell-tower-mental-health-response-largest-of-its-kind-in-europe

[3] 'Grenfell Tower Regeneration Project,' Royal Borough of Kensington and Chelsea, https://www.rbkc.gov.uk/idoxWAM/doc/Other-960664.pdf?extension=.pdf&id=960664&location=VOLUME2&contentType=application/pdf&pageCount=1

[4] 'Grenfell Tower Regeneration Project, October 2012,' Royal Borough of Kensington and Chelsea, https://www.rbkc.gov.uk/idoxWAM/doc/Other-960664.pdf?extension=.pdf&id=960664&location=VOLUME2&contentType=application/pdf&pageCount=1

[5] 'Grenfell Tower floorplan shows how 120 flats were packed into highrise,' 14 June 2017,The Telegraph, https://www.telegraph.co.uk/news/2017/06/14/grenfell-tower-floorplan-shows-120-flats-packed-highrise/

[6] Tom Symonds and Claire Ellison, 'Grenfell Tower cladding failed to meet standard', 5 April 2018, http://www.bbc.co.uk/news/uk-43558186

[7] E.g., Andrew Griffin, 'London fire: Mosques, churches and temples open doors to people caught up in Grenfell Tower', The Independent, 14 June 2017, https://www.independent.co.uk/news/uk/home-news/london-fire-help-mosques-churches-temples-grenfell-tower-injured-safe-how-to-a7789281.html

1
What the faith groups did

> *The first I heard of the fire was when our housemate woke me up and said, 'Grenfell Tower is burning, you need to come and see this.' Shortly after that, a friend of mine who lived in the Tower came to seek refuge having fled in their pyjamas. I stayed at home to look after them, but a colleague went, and our church was open by about 2.30am.*[1]

This first section explores both the immediate ways the faith groups responded to the fire, as well as longer-term responses, some of which are still on-going. As hinted at by the quotation above, this response took a number of forms: (1) the faith leaders very quickly opened the doors of their faith centres, and sometimes their homes, to those in need; (2) faith groups met the immediate practical needs of clothes, food, and water, predominantly through taking and distributing donations; (3) faith centres provided space and facilities for people to pray, reflect, or just sit quietly, away from the immediate crisis zone, as well as offering emotional and pastoral support and prayer; and (4), in the longer term, faith groups have been offering faith-sensitive support, including professional counselling and psychotherapy, prayer groups, and children's holiday camps, as well as practical and administrative support and moral support of the ongoing campaign effort.

The community

Lancaster West, the housing estate in which Grenfell Tower is situated, is in an area of extraordinary diversity. It lies in Notting Dale Ward, in the Royal Borough of Kensington and Chelsea. At the time of the last Census in 2011, Notting Dale had a population of about 8,500. Nearly a third – 29% – of households had a first language other than English and over four in ten – 41% – of people recorded their country of birth as other than the UK and Ireland (compared to 50% in the whole borough).[2] Just around the corner from Lancaster Road, over which Grenfell Tower stands, Clarendon Road, with its spacious early Victorian villas, stretches away to the south and some of the highest-valued real estate in Britain.

The vast majority of the people we spoke to in the course of this research described the Borough as an area of diversity "in every sense,"[3] and acknowledged the often extreme areas of economic and social inequality, leading to a sometimes "fragmented"[4] community facing "significant challenges."[5] Some people cited the asset-rich, cash-poor elderly residents in some large houses in the vicinity, "who've lived there since after the Second World War, but don't have any one to take them grocery shopping, and might be terribly lonely."[6] Others pointed out the number of local properties "bought as investments as second homes by foreign nationals, which lie empty most of the time."[7] Several interviewees referred to an "up-hill/down-hill divide," between the wealthier "top end of Notting Hill" and the poorer areas around the Latimer Road,[8] and in particular stated that the Council's plan for development of the Silchester Estate, which neighbours Lancaster West, amounts to "social cleansing."[9] For several interviewees, the fire at Grenfell "symbolises all that is wrong with society: inequality; lack of social engagement; a 'don't care', inhumane attitude,"[10] as one person put it. In the words of another, Grenfell "shows a fundamental failure to love our neighbour."[11]

That said, all our interviewees who spoke of the ethnic and cultural diversity of North Kensington presented that as a "source of strength."[12] When describing the local area, one interviewee, whilst acknowledging its challenges, asserted that it was still a very positive environment, and felt that "most people see it as a privilege to live here."[13] For the purposes of this report, it is significant that, as one interviewee put it:

> *The fact that the area is so ethnically diverse means that people here are more than usually religiously observant: people from immigrant communities, even to the second or third generation, tend to be more religiously observant than average in Britain.*[14]

Several others described the local community as "close-knit,"[15] and often suggested this was largely down to the "work of community groups,"[16] such as the Maxilla Children's Centre or St. Peter's Nursery,[17] amongst others. Moreover, we heard repeatedly in our interviews of relationships being made stronger as a result of working together during and since the crisis, and indeed that some previous divisions were, to some extent, "broken down"[18] by the fire and its aftermath.

The faith groups

As might be expected, the diversity of North Kensington is reflected in its faith groups. There are (at least) nine distinct faith groups (i.e., including different dominations of the major religions) in (at least) fifteen identifiable centres (e.g., places of worship, volunteer centres, and charity offices) within short walking distance of Grenfell Tower. Accordingly, the faith communities we spoke to included Anglicans, both Anglo-Catholic and evangelical, Methodists, Catholics, and people from Pentecostal, charismatic, and Free Churches, representatives of Muslim, Jewish, and Sikh groups, and local and national faith-based charities.

From these groups, our interviewees' familiarity with one another varied. On the whole, they had known each other, at least by sight, before the fire, and got to know each other better through their responses after Grenfell. One interviewee said:

> I didn't have any particular contact with the other faith groups [before the fire]. I knew the Sikh community at Shepherd's Bush a little, and I had some contact with the Catholic church nearest my church. I had met [one faith leader] when he moved in recently, and knew [another faith leader] in passing, but other than that, I didn't know many personally.[19]

Another interviewee remarked:

> I was aware of [some particular churches] as having strong, long-term relationships in the community, but there were others I didn't know of before.[20]

By contrast, some faith centres did have strong friendships and working relationships with others before the fire. One interviewee from a faith-based charity said that they had "a long-term relationship with [the local mosque]: as fellow Muslims, it's natural to partner with them."[21] This mosque had also been in partnership with a nearby synagogue, which had hosted an *iftar* (the evening meal for breaking the Ramadan fast) a couple of weeks before the fire, and would later go on to partner with them in holding children's holiday camps for the Grenfell community. We also heard of a church lending some computers to another following a break-in at the latter church's office, whilst a volunteer at a charity stated that "the [local] charities are all pretty united, and tend to work together well."[22] These links were especially helpful in co-ordinating the faith groups' responses, in both the immediate and longer terms, as will be explored more below.

The immediate response
Opening the doors

Across the board, faith centres were open quickly. According to news reports, the fire broke out on the fourth floor of Grenfell Tower at about 1am.[23] The emergency services received the first calls at that time, mostly from members of the Muslim community living in and around the Tower, who were awake to observe their Ramadan fast beginning at dawn (usually around 4:45 in mid-June, with the first prayers of the day performed from about two hours before that). Many of our interviewees' accounts followed a similar pattern: an ordinary night asleep at home, or awake to break the Ramadan fast, possibly aware of "disturbances from emergency vehicles,"[24] but not thinking much of it – until being wakened by a knock on the door, a phone call or a tweet.

One faith leader was woken in the early hours by a phone call from a member of his congregation whose friend was trapped in the Tower: "I checked the news straightaway, and the fire was the top headline on the BBC website. I was [at my church] in five minutes, and we were open by 9am."[25] The first another heard of it was when they "woke up as usual at about 6am, and saw I'd received a tweet from the BBC asking me to comment on a large fire in west London. I rang [a colleague] whose parish is there and went over as soon as I could."[26] Another said that due to hay fever – and what later turned out to be smoke inhalation – he'd had a disturbed night's sleep, and was woken in the early morning by "someone leaning on my doorbell. I went to answer it, and when I opened the door I found bits of Grenfell Tower [i.e., ash and fragments of the building's cladding] all over my doorstep."[27]

Almost without exception, the immediate reactions were very similar: urgently checking news outlets, making phone calls to friends in danger or to alert colleagues, rushing to their respective place of worship or work, opening doors to refugees and volunteers, announcing their presence on social media, and beginning the immediate hard graft of attending to the fire's survivors, volunteers, and mountains of donations. One Muslim interviewee we spoke to said:

Because it was Ramadan, I was up after midnight to pray, and began receiving texts from our staff saying, 'Grenfell Tower is burning, what shall we do?' I said, 'Open the doors [of their place of worship], welcome anyone who comes, we are to be open to all.' I then texted the Chair of our Board of Trustees and our network [alerting them to the fire and the faith centre's action], and one of our tweets saying '[We] are open' just went viral.[28]

The particular significance of Muslim communities being awake at night to observe the Ramadan fasting and prayers, and thus able to respond quickly to news of the fire, was summed up by one interviewee who said, "it being Ramadan saved lives."[29]

Another church leader told us how he was woken by a colleague just before 3am, and:

Went straight to the church, turned on the lights, lit the altar candles, and asked where the evacuation site was... I went to the Rugby Portobello Trust[30] *to see what was going on, and by the time we got back to the church there was at first a trickle, then a steady flow of [local] residents and volunteers, about 70 residents and 15 volunteers by 4.30am. People were bringing supplies of tea, breakfast, fruit, biscuits, and blankets. By 5.30am it was a full-scale operation.*[31]

One volunteer we spoke to said:

> *I heard of the fire on the news at about 5am or 6am ... I got to the Clement James centre at about 9.30am, taking stuff from our cupboards at home I thought might help. By the time I got there they were swamped with people and donations.*[32]

Practical response

Having opened their doors, at any point between 2.30am and 9am, the faith groups we spoke to frequently reported similar challenges and the nature of the responses to them. On a practical note, our interviewees all encountered an enormous number of volunteers and volume of donations from the earliest hours. Some faith leaders noted that whilst they initially opened their places of worship assuming they would be most useful as places of prayer, rest, and sanctuary, they very quickly became "pop-up donation sites,"[33] and local hubs for donations and volunteers seeking direction on how best to help. As one interviewee put it:

> *I thought on the morning [of the fire] that the best way our church could serve would be to comfort the survivors, and offer emotional and spiritual support, and we did do that, but after three hours of helping at my friend's church, when I came back, to my shock, there was a roadblock outside our church. The road was completely blocked with people trying to get to our church, and we were flooded with donations and volunteers.*[34]

Donations

As was well publicised at the time, our interviewees told us of the overwhelming generosity of the public in bringing donations. All the interviewees we spoke to who were on the ground at the time expressed their sincere gratitude to the members of the public who came forward to volunteer and to offer donations. In the words of one faith leader we spoke to:

The solidarity of the nation, expressed through social media, and the presence of the volunteers and donations, was so supportive to the survivors. That level of love speaks to people on a profound level.[35]

However, those interviewees who were in charge of their respective communities' responses also noted the logistical challenge presented by the sheer volume of the donations: some donations, such as blankets, weren't pressingly needed at the height of summer and "took up valuable space."[36] There was also an enormous contrast in the quality of the clothing donated, from "designer outfits"[37] to items "only suitable for the rag trade."[38] The variety of clothing along with the volume of donations meant that donation centres struggled to sort and distribute them without being overwhelmed. One faith leader described how a tweet from a prominent politician suggesting donations be taken to a particular faith centre went viral, and though the tweet was "well-meaning, it was unhelpful, as it led to us being inundated with donations; [we] were completely overwhelmed by stuff."[39] In response to this, a number of interviewees expressed the view that in any future crisis, money would be a more helpful donation than clothing, and we will explore this suggestion further in chapter 2.

The disposal of the surplus donations subsequently caused some controversy, both in the media and among those we spoke to. Participants were naturally concerned that all monies and supplies donated were either given to or utilised for those directly affected by the fire. Regarding the physical donations, we heard conflicting reports. Several faith groups told us that they still had significant reserves of donations either at their place of worship or in a storage facility. Indeed, a number of interviewees mentioned they had been given the use of storage space free of charge when the business owners heard the items were donations for the Grenfell community.[40] Others referred to a "pop-up shop" they had either seen or taken part in, in the weeks after the fire. In this, one faith group worked with some of the secular voluntary organisations to create a special "shopping experience" for the survivors of Grenfell:

We converted a space near The Westway Centre into a pop-up boutique, with rails of clothes organised by size, mirrors, and nice lighting, to make it a pleasant experience for the survivors. We invited them to come in and browse, and take away anything they liked for free.[41]

This faith leader reported that this had been a positive experience for the people who had taken part, and that it was felt to provide "a bit of normality amidst the trauma." Regarding the large volume of unclaimed donations, we heard several reports that these had been collected by the Red Cross, to be sold in their charity shops, with the proceeds being reserved for a Grenfell fund. As one interviewee said:

The amount of donated clothing was equivalent to five football fields, so dealing with it was a huge task. [...] The Red Cross partnered with the local authority and arranged, once the local needs were met, especially with new clothing, to take the surplus donations to their central depot. They sorted through these again, and sold them through their high-street charity shops and through the rag trade, if they were in such poor condition as to be unsellable. They were all marked that they were Grenfell donations, and the Red Cross were very careful that every penny from the sale of the donations were set aside for the victims and their families, nothing was to be taken away from them.[42]

This interviewee emphasised his gratitude to the Red Cross for being willing and able to "take on a major logistical headache," especially since "they came in for a bit of criticism for it, from people who feared they were taking away from the local community."

Food

The provision of food was also central to the relief effort. For many faith groups, hospitality is intrinsic to their life and work, and some faith groups' immediate response was to provide food and water. Some members of Muslim communities pointed out that:

> *We always have dates and bottles of water, especially in Ramadan when people have been fasting. We were able to give these to people in need straightaway, and as during Ramadan we host a nightly iftar and we have full-scale catering facilities, we were able to feed all the extra volunteers and survivors, both on the evening of 14 June and afterwards. We served hundreds of people a day for several weeks.*[43]

Other faith groups also served food throughout the relief effort and afterwards. Noting their gratitude for such swift and generous hospitality, one member of the local community said "the Sikhs came, and they did what they do: they served food."[44] While we heard a case of one faith group declining the offer of vegetarian food cooked by another faith group, on the grounds that it "might be ritually contaminated,"[45] on the whole there were only very positive reports of the faith groups cooking and eating together as fostering strong community support and making a significant difference to the relief effort.

Pastoral response

Amidst the immediate business of receiving and processing donations and directing volunteers, we also heard about the immediate "pastoral first-aid" the faith groups were able to offer those who had fled or witnessed the fire. One interviewee, who works in a faith-based charity that supports civil authorities and emergency services, particularly in the night-time economy and during crises, summed up their role as "to care for people in need, to listen and help them, and to offer prayer when appropriate."[46] Several faith leaders noted the unusual readiness of local residents to stop them and ask for prayer in the aftermath of the fire. As one faith leader described:

Local clergy made themselves available on the streets in the days immediately after the fire, offering to listen and pray with local people, if they wanted to. People really needed to talk.[47]

Another faith group, which works in partnership with the emergency services to provide pastoral care at the scene of an emergency, said of their work:

We allow them a space to talk about what they've seen, or just chat about the weather, or they just take a cup of tea and go. [The emergency services] are always glad to see us.[48]

Along with providing the refugees of Grenfell Tower and Walkways (the low-rise housing blocks around Grenfell Tower) with emotional and spiritual support, faith groups also reported being thrown together and united by the fire, ending up offering practical and spiritual support to each other. As one faith leader described:

As soon as I heard about the fire I went to my friend's church and started helping out with handling the donations and helping in any way I could. It wasn't until I got WhatsApp messages from my daughter saying that people were flooding our own church that I went back at lunchtime.[49]

Emotional and spiritual support was extended across faith differences. One Muslim interviewee described how a church leader joined some Muslim women in silent prayer at one place of worship acting as relief centre. The interviewee said, "I was so impressed and so grateful that [that church leader] did that, and I found it so comforting that we were all in the same boat."[50]

Faith groups and RBKC

We heard only positive reports of the work of the emergency services, both from faith leaders and civic personnel. As one faith leader described:

> *By the time I got to the site at 7am, I saw [off-duty] firefighters sitting on the ground, completely exhausted. Due to the strength of the fire and fears of the Tower collapsing, they were only allowed in to the Tower for 20 minutes at any one time.*[51]

Another faith leader with a history of partnering with the "blue light services" noted the emergency services' "really good, joined-up, multi-agency training: they are used to working with each other, fitting into a response well together."[52] This person also spoke of the professional development he had noticed in the emergency services since the 7/7 bombings. "They were great in handling 7/7, but they've had even better training, equipping, and resources since then."

Another interviewee stated that "The [London Fire Brigade] impress me every time I see them,"[53] whilst a fourth praised the emergency services' "humaneness, availability, patience, and professionalism."[54] This was particularly striking to many of our interviewees who noted that the same search and rescue teams that worked at Grenfell also attended the Manchester and London Bridge attacks in the same summer.[55]

The psychological repercussions of this were noted by several of the interviewees, one of whom said:

> I have a friend who is a firefighter, who attended Grenfell and needed to be signed off for a long time afterwards. [The emergency services] put themselves in physical and psychological danger in order to save lives.[56]

In this extraordinary context, a number of interviewees observed that the faith groups were called upon to the extent they were because people felt the lack of the Council's response. In the words of one interviewee, "the Council were not great – [the faith groups] had to fill in the gaps."[57] This was a widespread opinion, as the media coverage of the tragedy clearly showed, but it is also worth noting that several of our interviewees pointed out that Council or TMO (Tenant Management Organisation)[58] officers *may* have been present but were not visible due to a lack of recognisable uniform. One commented that "any council staff who might have been around did not have high-vis vests or walkie-talkies, so we wouldn't have known if they were there,"[59] suggesting that this apparent absence exacerbated any pre-existing negative perception of the Council amidst the local residents. Another interviewee said that in the face of unprecedented disaster:

> The Council collapsed. Groups like St Helen's Church, The ClementJames Centre, and The Westway Centre, 'became' the local government, as people lost trust in the Council. But people don't lose trust suddenly, it was lost before.[60]

The effect of this, apart from the considerable public anger, was to put more pressure on to the faith groups to pick up the slack. As one interviewee put it, discussing their perception that the faith groups bore the brunt of the relief effort, "surely it's for the state to step in in a crisis, churches and other faith groups can only support, not lead the effort themselves."[61]

Commenting on the pressures felt, and the ambiguous role of the Council, another interviewee said:

I was so desperate. I kept thinking that we just needed a saviour, someone to come and help and make things easier for us, but no one came, we just had to do it all ourselves and get to grips with the trauma of it all.[62]

It is worth noting, however, that the distinction between faith and voluntary groups, on the one hand, and the Council, on the other, was not always as clear cut as it seemed, and that there was, in fact, much positive interaction between the two. As one interviewee pointed, his faith centre:

Receives 50% of its funding from grants from local government. So the Council was present, in a way, in that [this centre] was in a much stronger position to respond because of financial backing from the local authority. If we hadn't had that, I'm not sure we would have been able to respond nearly as effectively as we did.[63]

Longer-term response

The faith groups' response did not end with the departure of the emergency vehicles. To some extent, the long-term response was due to the faith leaders' presence in their community, and as a natural development of their faith centres' work. Indeed, most faith leaders said that the impact Grenfell had had on their ministry was significant. As one interviewee put it, "Grenfell now takes up 95% of my day job. Work is much busier, but it is an honour to stand with the Grenfell community."[64]

All the faith leaders to whom we spoke expressed their conscious commitment to and solidarity with the Grenfell community. This was summed up by one interviewee who told us that he had said repeatedly to members of his congregation, "when the journalists and emergency services go, we'll still be here."[65] Another faith leader spoke of the dangers of "having a full stop" to faith groups' support of the Grenfell community:

> **When the journalists and emergency services go, we'll still be here.**

We can't just leave them now, when so many are still living in hotels and undergoing severe mental health issues, such as suicidal depression or PTSD. We can't have a 'full stop' to our support of them, just because the immediate crisis has passed. Our support must and will be ongoing for the foreseeable future.[66]

This interviewee gave the following example of their church's longer-term support of the Grenfell community:

Through the generosity of our congregation and the surrounding community, we have been able to maintain our presence in the Grenfell community by putting on special events, such as a Christmas dinner in late December. We invited people of all faiths from the Grenfell community, to enjoy a meal provided by a local hotel, with decorations provided by a top-end London florist, and even live reindeer outside, loaned from an entertainment company, for the kids to meet! Our choir sang carols, and we did silver service for the meal. The look on their faces when they came in was amazing: you could just see their shoulders relax just for a little while, as they understood that we had pulled this all together to make them feel special, cared for, and loved.

What the faith groups did

As well as expressing their gratitude for the continuing provision of such donations, many interviewees also highlighted the importance of financial rather than physical donations as enabling long-term support. Several interviewees described how a Muslim community had, through the generosity of financial donations, been able to employ professional counsellors and psychotherapists able to provide faith-sensitive mental health support. As one interviewee explained:

Some Muslims might not feel comfortable seeking help from a secular counsellor, who might not fully grasp their religious and cultural needs. Sometimes there are also cultural barriers which prevent Muslims from seeking support outside their immediate family communities, particularly from people of the opposite sex. Having male and female counsellors who are fluent in the Islamic tradition is therefore vital in supporting Muslims dealing with trauma.[67]

Along with talking therapies, we also heard of faith centres providing art therapy, particularly for children affected by Grenfell. In the words of interviewee:

Art therapy can be beneficial for everyone, and particularly for people and situations where language becomes difficult; for instance, when the client is a young child or has learning difficulties where they may not be able to express themselves through speech fully, or when English is not their first language, and they wouldn't be able to hold an in-depth conversation with a counsellor. It's also very useful in situations where the extent of the trauma means the client feels unable to put it into words.[68]

This person highlighted the significance of a Muslim centre running art therapy groups:

> *Art is usually a lower priority amongst immigrant communities, where the sciences tend to be more highly prized. For a Muslim community to be offering art therapy is a visionary decision.*

This person described the art therapy groups run by this faith centre where children had initially:

> *Just used the wet materials, like pouring out paint onto paper, or using clay. Usually this demonstrates a need for catharsis, that they are somehow pouring out their pain and trauma, and feeling a release with making 'mess.'*

Since running these groups, this person, along with others at different groups, had noticed children:

> *Coming to terms with what happened through playing with first aid kits and pretending to be paramedics. At one recent session, one child spent the whole time just zipping and unzipping a first aid kit; the repetition seemed to soothe them.*

Another interviewee involved with faith-based children's work described how:

> *Children often play 'Mummies and Daddies' or 'Doctors and Nurses', but since Grenfell we noticed them playing 'Fire-fighters and Paramedics', as a way of imitating what they saw and of coming to terms with it.*[69]

We also heard of faith groups running joint events for the Grenfell community. We heard of one case where faith centres of different religions came together to run a holiday camp for 'Grenfell kids'. As one interviewee explained:

> *Sadly, Grenfell is likely to be a dominating event influencing the rest of the lives of the children in the community. We wanted to offer an environment where being a 'Grenfell kid' could be*

more than a label denoting a heavy trauma, but somehow redeemed into being part of a positive, supportive community, and a source of strength. Of course, nothing can ever fully make up for or take away from the horror of what happened, but we hope, in time, there might be some positives amid the trauma.[70]

A colleague of this interviewee described how they had run a faith-sensitive children's holiday camp:

> **We wanted to offer an environment where being a 'Grenfell kid' could be more than a label denoting a heavy trauma, but somehow redeemed into being part of a positive, supportive community, and a source of strength.**

> *We offered a non-residential course during half-term where children aged six to eleven could come and be spoiled a bit. We taught them circus skills, we did fun science experiments, we took them on a trip to a soft-play centre. The kids all smiled from start to finish and we had really positive feedback from their parents, many of whom told us they seemed a lot more settled and well-behaved at home.*[71]

This interviewee told us they were planning to run similar events for the foreseeable future, to offer a source of security and stability for the children involved, as well as providing respite for the children's parents. His colleague, who helped to run the camp, told us that:

> *To be sensitive to the needs of the Grenfell kids we made sure we had religiously-permissible food, and also we had a higher than usual ratio of staff to children – it was one member of staff to every two children – and we made sure that all the games were as gentle and as quiet as possible, to avoid the children being overwhelmed.*[72]

This interviewee, along with many others, highlighted the importance of financial rather than physical donations as enabling this kind of longer-term support, and of subsidising and enabling other initiatives responding to the needs of the community.

The ongoing support has not been limited to children's work. One faith leader told us of a prayer group set up in her faith centre for mothers affected by Grenfell. This person described how often parents, especially mothers, bear the brunt of providing emotional support for their families, and how often they have been told to "stay strong for the children."[73] Recognising the toll this 'stiff upper lip approach' could take on mothers in the community, this faith centre set up a prayer and support group for mothers, where:

> *Mothers who are in any way affected by Grenfell can come and relax, cry if they need to, and receive peer support and prayer if they want it. It's a safe place for them to come and be honest about how Grenfell affects them, without needing to be 'strong' for their families.*

This interviewee commented that the group has been well attended and that "as a mother who is affected by Grenfell myself, I'm eligible to attend, and I do when I can."

On the whole, we heard that the ongoing support efforts have been well attended. Occasionally, however, there has been less demand for specific groups. We heard of one art class, subsidised by donations, open for young people to attend for free. However, perhaps due to a lack of demand amongst local teens and young people, or unsuccessful advertising, the faith leader at the centre where it was to be held told us "we didn't get enough people signing up. So we cancelled it, and donated the funds to another voluntary centre running events for young people affected by Grenfell."[74] This experience was a minority one, however, and most interviewees told us that the faith centres' offers of support had been warmly received.

Conclusion

In what we heard of the efficacy of the faith groups' immediate response, three key themes emerged. These were (1) the speed with which faith centres opened their doors; (2) the practical ways in which faith groups met the most pressing needs, by distributing food and clothing to those who had fled with literally nothing more than the clothes they were wearing; and (3) the pastoral response, both in the short-term provision of space for rest, prayer, and respite, and in the longer term, of offering faith-sensitive counselling and rehabilitation groups of all kinds.

In contrast to this response, we also heard, from many perspectives, about the challenges of relating to statutory bodies, and the extent to which faith groups felt compelled to make up for the perceived shortfall of aid and organisation from local and national authorities. How the faith groups were placed to do so and what facilitated their response will be explored in the following chapter.

[1] Interview #withheld

[2] 'Notting Dale Ward Profile', Royal Borough of Kensington and Chelsea, https://www.rbkc.gov.uk/pdf/Notting%20Daledata.pdf

[3] Interview #13

[4] Interview #1

[5] Interview #15

[6] Interview #4

[7] Interview #11

[8] Interview #11

[9] Interview #4

[10] Interview #28

[11] Interview #1

[12] Interview #15

[13] Interview #17

[14] Interview #19

[15] Interview #18

[16] Interview #19

[17] St. Peter's Nursery is based at the wealthier 'top end' of Notting Hill, and as such, as one interviewee pointed out, tends not to serve the poorer community closer to Grenfell Tower. However, another interviewee pointed out that "there's hardly any child in Notting Hill who didn't go to St. Peter's at some point, or knows someone who did," (Interview #11), so whilst its catchment area may not normally include the immediate community around Grenfell, the effects it creates of community cohesion are more widespread.

[18] Interview #2

[19] Interview #10

[20] Interview #5

[21] Interview #15

[22] Interview #18

[23] Benjamin Kentish, 'Grenfell Tower fire caused by faulty fridge on fourth floor, reports suggest', The Independent, 16 June 2017. https://www.independent.co.uk/news/uk/home-news/grenfell-tower-cause-fridge-faulty-fourth-floor-london-kensington-disaster-latest-a7792566.html

[24] Interview #17

[25] Interview #4

[26] Interview #1

[27] Interview #17

What the faith groups did

[28] Interview #2

[29] Interview #15

[30] A local charity which works with children, young people, and families, helping them to "overcome disadvantages [of North Kensington's] much higher than average levels of burglary, street crimes and violent attacks as well as drug and alcohol abuse [...] by providing a positive alternative to a life of crime, deprivation and social exclusion." 'Where We Work', The Rugby Portobello Trust, http://www.rugbyportobello.org.uk/where_we_work.php

[31] Interview #10

[32] Interview #18

[33] Interview #13

[34] Interview #26

[35] Interview #13

[36] Interview #21

[37] Interview #3

[38] Interview #29

[39] Interview #29

[40] e.g., Interview #26

[41] Interview #13

[42] Interview #29. See Laura Oakley, 'Shop for Grenfell: Why we're turning donations into cash', British Red Cross Blog, 28 June 2017, http://blogs.redcross.org.uk/appeals/2017/06/shop-grenfell-turning-donations-cash/

[43] Interview #2

[44] Interview #28

[45] Interview #22

[46] Interview #16

[47] Interview #1

[48] Interview #24

[49] Interview #26

[50] Interview #15

[51] Interview #1

[52] Interview #23

[53] Interview #24

[54] Interview #13

[55] We heard this from several interviewees but have not been able to verify it independently.

[56] Interview #6

[57] Interview #19

[58] Tenant Management Organisations were set up under the UK Government's Housing (Right to Manage) Regulations 1994, to enable residents of council housing or housing association homes in the UK to take over responsibility for the running of their homes. Subsequently, RBKC took over the management of its homes from the TMO on 1 March 2018.

[59] Interview #4

[60] Interview #21

[61] Interview #17

[62] Interview #13

[63] Interview #27

[64] Interview #2

[65] Interview #7

[66] Interview #26

[67] Interview #2

[68] Interview #8

[69] Interview #11

[70] Interview #8

[71] Interview #6

[72] Interview #8

[73] Interview #13

[74] Interview #17

2
How they were able to do it

Having looked at *what* the faith groups did in their immediate and longer term responses to the fire, this section explores *how* the faith groups were able to respond effectively and swiftly to the crisis: what was it about them that enabled them to react in the way they did?

On the whole, three main reasons emerged. These were (1) the trust the faith groups had built up amongst the community; (2) the fact they had secure spaces that could be used at short notice; and (3) the combination of recognised protocols and networks with the capacity to be flexible and 'improvise' according to needs as they emerged. We look at each of these in turn.

Trust

Longevity

Many of our interviewees cited the length of time faith leaders or centres had been in the area as enabling the community's trust in them. One faith group reported having served in war and crisis zones "since being in the trenches of the First World War,"[1] and suggested that this long-standing presence facilitated civic, voluntary, and other faith groups' trust in them, while also building up their expertise and ability to respond skilfully.

Most of the faith groups' leaders had been in post for at least five years, with most of the centres themselves having been present in the area for around 50-100 years. More than simple longevity, however, we heard repeatedly that in that time, faith centres had been running faith-sensitive initiatives and social work that had made a significant difference in the community. These included but were not limited to running or supporting local faith schools, holding prayer groups and Bible or Qur'an study groups, providing homework clubs and coaching to help school-leavers apply to university, and offering courses on computer skills or English as a foreign language.

Living in the community

Another feature of the faith leaders' lives and work that contributed to the sense of trust was the fact that most of the leaders to whom we spoke lived (and live) in or very near the community around Grenfell. This meant, first, that they were often seen as having a natural empathy with the concerns and lives of members of their faith centres – in the words of one interviewee, "it's our home, not just our workplace,"[2] – and second, that they were able to be present and to open their doors within a very short time of hearing of the fire.[3]

This local knowledge was especially helpful when it came to helping the emergency services who did not know the area so well. Several of our interviewees pointed out that due to the scale of the disaster, extra personnel needed to be drafted in to support the local teams. In the words of one interviewee, a local person who was hampered in getting to his faith centre due to the number of roads closed by the cordon:

They didn't know the streets around the cordon, so they couldn't tell us how to get to the other side. It wasn't their fault at all, they were very helpful otherwise, but the fact they didn't know the area meant we were slowed down in reaching the [faith centres] we were trying to help.[4]

Networks

The combination of these two elements – presence and longevity – meant that most faith leaders and groups had developed extensive and trusted networks in the local community. Neighbours and members of faith communities were able to say to their respective faith leaders, "you've got to get yourself down here,"[5] because they had their contact details *and* a level of trust whereby they knew their faith leaders would be ready and willing to help in a crisis.

For instance, one of our interviewees who volunteered at a community centre went straight there on the morning of the fire, having been alerted via Twitter that they were open. She knew from former experience that this centre would be offering skilful and appropriate help in whatever ways it could. When asked why both survivors and volunteers might turn to faith groups as their first port of call, almost all interviewees answered, as one person put it, that:

> *Churches and mosques have a historical association of being a safe haven. [...] People also like to go where they know people already; I've been in my job for the last nine years, and we found [survivors] asking for [members of staff] by name during the crisis, because they wanted help from someone they knew already.*[6]

The role of pre-existing relationships in a crisis, and the help they can provide, will be explored further in chapter 3.

Space

Along with the historical and personal bonds faith groups had developed in their communities, many interviewees highlighted another *practical* explanation for the efficacy of the faith groups' response, namely the available space in their buildings.

As noted above, this turned out to be extremely useful in the circumstances. It enabled the faith groups to receive and store donations, to prepare drinks and food, to offer somewhere to rest and recuperate, and to reflect and to grieve in.

This is an important factor, and perhaps one that is too infrequently recognised. 'Community' is an overwhelmingly positive word in our society, applied to all manner of things, from villages to social media groups. However, community that fully serves people, in all their messy, varied, material and spiritual needs, requires secure, sheltered, well-equipped, and ideally well-staffed physical space. The fact that the faith groups around Grenfell were able to supply this proved to be very significant, prompting one interviewee to go as far as to suggest that the *only* reason refugees and volunteers turned to the faith groups was "because they had the space, and they were physically there, local in the community."[7]

Balance of professionalism and flexibility

The final explanation we heard for the efficacy of the faith groups' response was the balance of professional protocols in place with the willingness and capacity to be flexible when necessary. Several members of members of a church that hosted a service of prayer and lament on Friday 16 June and set up a charity fund in about 24 hours suggested that the reason they were able to act so swiftly was because, "We're three things in one: a church, a hall [which is a functioning venue], and a playgroup."[8]

Another interviewee pointed out that the fact they have "a number of employed, full time staff means we have a contact list of people we know are willing to come out if we get in touch with them, and we're able to move quickly in organising things."[9] This was in contrast to concerns raised by almost all interviewees over the numbers of:

Spontaneous volunteers – [those] very kind-hearted, well-meaning people who came to help but sometimes didn't know how best to help, whom we couldn't verify or know if they had DBS checks, and who thus presented a serious safeguarding issue [especially] for the people most in need of help.[10]

The fact that all faith centres had at least a few (and sometimes many) members of appropriately-trained staff with DBS checks in place meant, for our interviewees, that they were able to rely on them and avoid placing "spontaneous volunteers" in potentially dangerous situations. Moreover, through their established protocols, many faith centres were also able to ensure their staff and networks received suitable debriefing and pastoral care after the initial crisis phase. One interviewee said, "we always have a debrief for the team attending any event [to offer pastoral assistance], with qualified counsellors. After [Grenfell] we had a more intense debrief with outside experts."[11]

The necessity for this more thorough debrief becomes starkly apparent in light of this interviewee's comment that some members of his faith group who attended the Aberfan disaster in 1966, are still sometimes "triggered", (i.e., experience sudden, serious, psychological difficulties) following that. He raised a concern that smaller groups, without an available network of professional psychological and pastoral care, would find it harder to resource teams responding to a crisis, especially in the long term.[12]

That noted, many interviewees also pointed out that along with professional and legal protocols and frameworks, faith groups were able to be more flexible in their approach. In the words of one person, "We could think on our feet, and weren't tied to having to sign things off all the time."[13] Another interviewee summed it up in saying "we wouldn't be unwise or foolish, but we could be flexible – we answer to a higher authority than bureaucracy."[14] An interviewee who worked at a faith-based charity spoke of the importance of having flexibility and sensitivity in the way case workers were able to support families. This interviewee told us:

> *Often [local government] case workers can only work nine to five, and aren't able to support families outside that time. We made sure we had enough staff and resources to be on hand to help 24/7, and I think our families [the charity supported] were appreciative of that.*[15]

Two other interviewees told us how they worked together in compiling a list of local people they personally knew or could vouch for, who had offered accommodation in their homes to displaced families. One of these people said:

> *We made it clear to [displaced] people that we hadn't done any formal checks, but that these were people we knew or had connections to, and who'd offered accommodation in their homes. Someone from the Council told us to stop, but a few families took up the offer, and I heard later it went well.*[16]

This ability to respond directly to the community's needs as they presented was a source of satisfaction to many of our interviewees. One interviewee described how his faith centre tried to "return to our usual framework as soon as possible," to provide continuity to the people it served, "whilst also providing space for new needs Grenfell has created. Those needs, and our response to them, are continuing to today."[17]

Conclusion

We heard a good deal about the strengths of the faith groups' response. That they tended to be rooted and known in their communities through a combination of long service and living in or near the area significantly boosted their ability to respond quickly and helpfully. We also heard of more practical factors that facilitated the faith groups' response, such as available building space, and pre-existing relationships and communication networks, as well as links to broader city- or nation-wide groups and denominational support.

Given the unprecedented scale of the crisis, and that a crisis is, by definition, chaotic and stressful,[18] the vast majority of interviewees expressed the view that their faith groups and centres could not reasonably be expected to react differently, or 'better' than they did. That said, many interviewees noted that had they not been so flooded with donations and "spontaneous volunteers", and more able to decline both when at capacity, their response might have felt calmer and more manageable.

This, and other practical points which our interviewees had noted during and after the disaster, and which they believed would be useful for faith and voluntary groups against future crises, will be detailed further in the final chapter, to which we now turn.

How they were able to do it

1. Interview #29
2. Interview #5
3. Interview #4, #5
4. Interview #7
5. Interview #28
6. Interview #19
7. Interview #28
8. Interview #11
9. Interview #9
10. Interview #29
11. Interview #29
12. Interview #29
13. Interview #19
14. Interview #13
15. Interview #15
16. Interview #21
17. Interview #29
18. Interview #16

3
Lessons from Grenfell

Having looked at *what* the faith groups did in response to Grenfell, and *how* they were able to respond in the ways they did, this final chapter explores what we can learn from the experience. To re-iterate, this report looks at one particular element of the Grenfell fire, and is not intended to be a full analysis of its causes, or even a comprehensive guide to how faith groups should respond to any potential tragedy in the future. As one interviewee told us candidly, "if a crisis occurred on my doorstep, my first reaction would not be to go back into my office and pull down a Theos report!"[1] Rather, our focus and interests are narrowly on what the faith groups did, how they did it, and what can be learned from it.

Many of our interviewees made remarks to the effect that they thought the scale of the fire and the subsequent volunteer effort was unprecedented in British peacetime, and thus that it would have been impossible to produce a 'perfect' response to the crisis. In spite, or perhaps because, of that the majority of our interviewees could talk to us about various lessons they had learnt through their response and that of others, and which they felt would be useful in case of future crises. These lessons broadly fell in to three themes: (1) be prepared, (2) be visible, and (3) be flexible.

1 Preparation

As noted, most interviewees acknowledged that no reasonable preparation could fully prepare communities and faith groups for a tragedy on the scale of Grenfell. Our interviewees did, however, outline some groundwork that had, or would, put them in the best possible position to respond to an emergency, particularly in terms of enhancing community cohesion ahead of time. These were (A) to practise an emergency response, (B) to utilise existing networks to their fullest, and (C) to foster new networks ahead of time.

A Practise your response

We heard from several interviewees about the importance of, what one called, adequate "preparation in peacetime",[2] i.e., before any crisis occurs. This could take a form similar to school fire drills, with an emphasis on "everyone involved knowing their role,"[3] and their response to any shared issues which might come out in an emergency. Other interviewees highlighted the need for faith and voluntary groups to be forewarned on other practical issues such as which church halls were available to use as collection or mustering points to encourage the swiftest possible response on the day of any crisis.[4] As one interviewee put it:

> *In each faith group there is most likely someone who emerges as the natural point person. Sometimes it's the faith leader, but not always. This person needs to have the names and phone numbers of the point people in other local faith groups, and vice versa. Each needs to know what the other can offer.*[5]

It was hoped that the fire at Grenfell could start a national conversation on what voluntary and faith groups could bring to any crisis on a similar scale, and that each faith group in a community would have a clear understanding of their own capacity and resources, and how that related to the local context.

B Use your networks

A number of interviewees raised concerns about possible safeguarding issues in the light of the huge numbers of spontaneous volunteers, and particularly the "grotesque disaster tourists,"[6] i.e., people who visited the site out of curiosity rather than a wish to help, "taking selfies"[7] rather than bringing donations.

To protect against this, several interviewees emphasised the importance of faith centres developing a detailed list of possible volunteers, and ensuring adequate training and qualification beforehand. As one faith leader put it, the response to Grenfell showed "the depth and breadth of the church,"[8] in the numbers of people willing and able to volunteer in faith groups' relief efforts.

In order to harness this most effectively, a number of volunteers suggested faith or volunteer centres hold a database of volunteers on whom they could call in a crisis. As one interviewee, whose faith group has a long history of working in crisis situations, put it:

Of course people are nervous of bureaucracy, but training volunteers to basic national standards needn't be onerous. We're not talking about heavy guidelines but basic principles of best practice.[9]

The necessity of such a database was highlighted by this interviewee and several others who reported a small but significant number of individuals, "who were not there to help, but for their own ends,"[10] "blagging their way in [to a relief centre], pretending to be a [registered] volunteer,"[11] or even, in some cases, survivors.[12] As another faith leader familiar with crisis situations put it, "it's a disaster zone, not a plaything. We need strong cordons to keep certain people out."[13]

It was hoped that if a database of trained volunteers was prepared and managed effectively, any faith or volunteer centre would be able politely but firmly to decline the offer of assistance from spontaneous volunteers, who might not have received adequate safeguarding or pastoral training, thus minimising unnecessary overcrowding of any relief centre.[14]

Another practical suggestion was made by an interviewee who had set up a charity fund in response to the fire within 24 hours:

Almost all churches or faith centres will have an official bank account. It should be possible, as we did, to create another account, under the same charity number, in case of emergency. This account could be kept dormant, and untitled, until it was needed, whereupon it would be very quick to 'flip the switch', give it a specific name relevant to the crisis, and have it open for donations.[15]

This interviewee specified that he had minimised the potential for fraud by ensuring the account could only receive payments, and not release them without going through due protocol in the faith centre's office. He also pointed out that the account name had deliberately referred to being for use in the North Kensington area, to allow the funds to be used to address the long-term needs of the Grenfell community in whichever way they were needed, not only for specific needs such as accommodation or education. We heard from several interviewees that this fund and others had been helpful in subsidising ongoing relief efforts, such as children's groups or counselling sessions for those affected by Grenfell.

Some faith leaders emphasised the importance of getting to know their staff and volunteers well, in order to harness any skills or experience that might be useful in a crisis, but which fall outside the remit of their usual work. One leader described a member of the Council staff who came to pass on some information, but during their conversation:

> *Mentioned she had previous experience in disaster relief and could therefore have been used in a more strategic role than the one she had been given. [...] Because she was not able to assume a disaster response role within the Council response that would have made use of her previous experience, she could not utilise that experience.*[16]

This interviewee suggested that faith groups and statutory bodies "make full use of the skills of people working with them" and be prepared to ask and train certain members of staff to step in to different roles in case of emergency.

C Foster new networks

Around half our interviewees registered frustration that statutory authorities did not fully appreciate the extent of faith groups' capacity to help during the crisis. This was deemed particularly necessary in a crisis, like Grenfell, so large and traumatic that it would stretch any local authority's usual disaster planning preparation.[17] These interviewees were strongly in favour of faith groups working *with* their respective local authority to make the authority fully aware of what the faith groups were able to offer in terms of volunteers, space, and relevant skills.

Several interviewees asked, in the words of one faith leader, "Were the local authorities aware of the help faith groups could give in a crisis, and had they incorporated that into their contingency planning? If not, why not?"[18] Another interviewee registered a similar frustration that local authorities seemed not to have considered what faith groups could offer, but said, "in the future, faith groups should be proactive, and make their Council aware of how we could help in a crisis."[19] One interviewee confirmed that there were indeed contingency plans:

> *[My faith centre] is included in the contingency plans for a disaster in my immediate area, which is a short distance from Grenfell. I'm sure that RBKC will have had contingency plans for Notting Dale Ward, and included the faith groups in that – though whether all sides were aware of that is a different matter.*[20]

Other interviewees told us of the importance of developing new relationships with other faith groups in their community. Several faith leaders put their efficacy down largely to a history of positive involvement in their communities. As one said:

> *We've had a [faith centre] in the community for over 100 years. [...] We were there before the fire, we were there during it, and we'll be there afterwards. That's helped people to trust us.*[21]

Others pointed out the natural empathy which faith groups have with one another as "sharing similar values."[22] From this, it was felt that faith groups could participate in localised network/ knowledge sharing. One faith leader told us how he had been a member of a multi-faith Major Incident Planning group, in partnership with the police force and other local faith groups elsewhere in London in his previous post.[23] This interviewee acknowledged the heavy administrative burden this had placed on him and others participating, yet he felt it was still a beneficial effort, especially during the 7/7 bombings when the partnership had proved "invaluable." He said that whilst he was glad to be involved, the bureaucracy needed, particularly in keeping new members informed of any changes to procedure or local infrastructure, means that "the driving energy for these groups must come from the local Council, not predominantly the faith groups."[24] Another interviewee acknowledged that many people are "rightly terrified of bureaucracy, but ideally, any knowledge-sharing enterprise doesn't have to be onerous."[25]

2   Be visible

A large proportion of our interviewees registered the importance of their visibility as a way of establishing trust among the community and thus of helping the relief effort. For instance, of those Christian leaders interviewed from denominations which use clerical collars, all mentioned that they intentionally wore them during the relief effort, even those who, from personal preference, tend not to wear theirs often. As one faith leader explained, a "clerical collar [is] a must for disasters and serious pastoral situations,"[26] and in the words of another, "if you're wearing a dog collar, people naturally come up and talk to you."[27]

As mentioned above, very occasionally this caused confusion when local residents saw "someone in a dog collar and assumed I knew what was going on."[28] However, the person who experienced this, along with others, also reported some local residents identifying him as a Christian minister due to his clothing, and approaching him for pastoral support and prayer.

Another interviewee, from a faith-based charity, noted that they were "on the ground before the Council – we just got on with things," and that this swift and visible action facilitated both the efficiency of their response and the process of gaining the trust of the people they served.[29]

3   Be flexible

Many of the people we spoke to reported faith and volunteer groups' ability to be flexible as a key strength in a crisis. As one person put it, "any prepared guidelines must always be open to change in a crisis,"[30] and in the words of another, "the Church is well placed to create an improvised hierarchy in a crisis [with a designated leader] – which is not naturally the expertise of a local authority."[31] Another person described their faith centre's ability to react swiftly to the crisis as it unfolded, and to communicate its needs as they developed:

> *The volunteers did a fantastic job of sorting through and distributing the donations. When things came up which we needed, like art supplies for the children to play with, we tweeted about it, and people saw that and came straightaway with what we'd said we needed.*[32]

Some interviewees expressed this in more spiritual terms. As one faith leader said:

> *So often during the crisis there would be something that we needed, and just as soon as I noticed that and was wondering where to get it, someone would walk in and offer just what we needed, like certain foods or the use of a storage facility. It was such an answer to prayer.*[33]

Financial donations

Regarding these needs, several people told us that monetary donations were more useful than clothing or food donations:

> *As money can be put towards any need, whereas physical donations of food or toiletries only serve certain needs, and take a huge amount of effort to manage and sort them.*[34]

Indeed, flexibility was deliberately incorporated into some funds set up after the crisis, to allow the money to be used "wherever it was needed in the Grenfell community after the crisis, not just specifically for one set of needs."[35]

This was particularly important for our interviewees when the scale of the crisis is borne in mind. A large number of people relayed reports that the medical and psychological needs of the Grenfell community constitute the greatest challenge of its kind to the NHS since its inception and the largest in Europe today, particularly in terms of mental health support,[36] with others reporting estimates that the fire had in some way affected 20,000 people, who will be in need of medical or psychological support in the immediate to further future.[37] In that context, the ability to resource a variety of pressing needs and longer-term projects through financial donations rather than food or clothing becomes eminently practical.

Offers of help

Most faith leaders expressed the hope that in future there would be greater communication between faith groups and local authorities, in order that everyone would be best placed to help the others in time of need. Some faith leaders noted particular offers of help they had taken up during the crisis which had significantly aided their response effort.

One faith leader told us how their area office had lent them the services of a secretary to assist with administration "at any point over those two weeks" that this faith leader was on the ground at Grenfell.[38] Another faith leader accepted the help of a volunteer who:

Came in, made a spreadsheet of contact details, answered the phone, and I was able to slow down for the first time.[...] A few weeks later, through the generosity of the church body, I was loaned the services of a professional PA.[39]

The importance of this administrative support should not be underestimated. This faith leader, along with almost every other interviewee, emphasised how significant was Grenfell's impact on the staff and volunteers responding to it. She described the first days as weeks "passing in a blur; it felt as if the world had arrived." As noted above, the majority of people we spoke to lived in the immediate community, and all had strong links there. Thus, in this faith leader's words, the crisis "happened to us, not just people far away. We, the local community, are the part of the walking wounded ourselves. [...] We cannot underestimate the effect on our staff."

The effect for this faith leader in practical terms, aside from the considerable psychological and emotional stress, was being "glued" to her mobile phone: "as I was the only one who had all the admin information, I couldn't put the phone down for a second before it rang again." Accordingly, the administrative help from the volunteer and PA allowed this faith leader not only to take a necessary day off once a week, but also allowed her to attend to other needs in her faith centre uninterrupted by constant telephone calls.

Others related the offers of help from high street brands, not just donations of food and clothing "worth many thousands of pounds"[40] but of help with logistics. In the words of one interviewee, "[the brand] said, 'We do logistics every day, why should you have to learn new skills right now, when we can help you with it?'"[41]

Regarding the apparent lack of statutory logistical planning, some interviewees expressed the view that the Council's decision not to bring in Gold Command, (the highest level of command and authority of the emergency services in a crisis situation)[42] as soon as possible was "criminally negligent",[43] and that in future, crises on the scale of Grenfell should receive Gold Command support as a matter of course.

Another interviewee said that it would be unsustainable for any local authority to constantly maintain adequate resources for such an extraordinary event, "that's why the London Gold system is there, so you can tap in to something else and have wider support when you need it."[44] As one interviewee put it, "I have been in war zones, but I've not seen anything comparable to Grenfell. It was a national disaster, [so] it is for the government to take charge."[45]

Person-centred & religiously sensitive pastoral care

Lastly, we heard about the importance of providing religiously- and culturally-sensitive pastoral care. In particular, given the large number of Muslim families affected by the fire (one interviewee suggested at least 65% of households in the tower were Muslim families[46]), we heard about specific needs which might otherwise not have been met but by faith-sensitive volunteers.

One Muslim interviewee explained the difficulties that Muslim families faced when fleeing from the fire, and being met by non-Muslim volunteers, many of whom pressed the refugees into breaking their fast.

> *They meant well, and of course, in an emergency [a Muslim] can make up their fast at a later date, but what [the non-Muslim volunteers] didn't understand was the Muslim belief that the prayer of someone fasting is never rejected by God.*[47]

Thus, our interviewee suggested that it would not have been culturally appropriate to encourage someone to break their fast, if it was a source of comfort to them and if it could be seen to aiding the efficacy of their prayers. This person also spoke of the importance of sourcing culturally-appropriate clothing for Muslims, such as loose dresses or headscarves: "the mosque had these in storage anyway – we could go straight to the families [in temporary accommodation] and deliver what they needed."

Being prepared to visit bereaved families on their terms and out of hours was not restricted to this faith group.[48] Another interviewee from a faith-based charity explained how their grounding in faith-orientated social work enabled them to provide:

> *Culturally and religiously sensitive funerals [to the victims of the fire], which were person-centred in advocating the needs of the next of kin [...] We meet people where they are at, both literally and metaphorically.*[49]

This interviewee told us of various customs at Muslim funerals which were problematic after Grenfell. For instance, it is traditional amongst Muslim communities to bury the deceased in a white shroud rather than a coffin. As our interviewee put it:

> *After Grenfell, sometimes the bodies were not intact, so a shroud would not have been appropriate to contain the remains. So we arranged for these families to bury their loved ones in a white coffin instead, to maintain the dignity of the deceased.*[50]

This interviewee also mentioned the significant number of "partners" – mosques, undertakers, and burial sites – that offered their services free of charge or heavily subsidised, in order to support the work of his charity, and more importantly, as a way of offering their condolences to the bereaved. This charity had also advertised being available to help non-Muslim families after Grenfell, and at the time of writing, had arranged at least one Christian funeral and burial.

For any person of faith, of which there are more than average in the Grenfell community, "prayer is a source of strength,"[51] and all our interviewees expressed the significance of faith during the crisis. However, for many of our interviewees, spiritual needs can become even more pressing when they are in a minority, and it was their express hope that the needs and customs of any and all faith communities could be supported during any future event like Grenfell.

Conclusion

From their experience in responding to Grenfell, as well as from their years of ministry experience, our interviewees suggested a variety of ways communities can best report to a crisis. Broadly, these fell into the themes of being (1) prepared, (2) visible, and (3) flexible.

Preparation could take the form of practice drills and information-sharing, as well as, more broadly, concerted efforts to develop and cultivate strong, sincere relationships with other local and national faith groups and local authorities.

The necessity of visibility, through uniform and identification, was explained not only in terms of establishing the 'point-person' in any faith or voluntary centre, but also as a means of improving morale by making it clear to the community in crisis which faith, voluntary or statutory groups are present and in solidarity with them.

Finally, the need to be flexible was detailed through being specific and firm about communities' needs as they develop, and able politely to discourage the delivery of unnecessary donations, to avoid being overwhelmed and hindered in the provision of aid.

To this end, most interviewees felt that financial donations were the most helpful in a crisis, taking up no space and being able to be used for any necessary purpose. Coherent systems, e.g., bank accounts or collection buckets, for managing these donations could also be prepared in advance, and updated to reflect the specific needs of a crisis as it develops.

Along with asserting their needs, faith groups expressed their sincere gratitude for offers of help which met these needs, such as administrative or pastoral assistance. Accordingly, interviewees expressed the hope that in any future crisis, faith groups would be able to be specific in stating their needs and open to all appropriate offers of help.

Lastly, interviewees emphasised the wisdom and insight faith groups have of the cultural and spiritual needs of people of faith – even of those outside their usual faith communities. It was strongly hoped that faith groups would make themselves available to advise and support secular voluntary groups and statutory authorities in the best ways to help and care for individuals and communities of faith, and that in these ways, the Grenfell Tower fire might bring about genuine, positive change in our society today.

1. Interview #6
2. Interview #29
3. Interview #20
4. Interview #10
5. Interview #13
6. Interview #16
7. Interview #29
8. Interview #13
9. Interview #29
10. Interview #17
11. Interview #29
12. Interview #7
13. Interview #24
14. Interviews #24, #16, #29
15. Interview #9
16. Interview #13
17. Interview #24
18. Interview #7
19. Interview #15
20. Interview #30
21. Interview #29
22. Interview #22
23. Interview #10
24. Interview #10
25. Interview #21
26. Interview #10
27. Interview #17
28. Interview #14
29. Interview #15, 26
30. Interview #23
31. Interview #17
32. Interview #18
33. Interview #26
34. Interview #29
35. Interview #1

[36] Interview #4. "The mental health response following the Grenfell Tower fire is the biggest operation of its kind in Europe, a doctor has said, with the number of people affected likely to exceed 11,000." Press Association, 'Grenfell Tower mental health response 'largest of its kind in Europe'", The Guardian, 30 October 2017, https://www.theguardian.com/uk-news/2017/oct/30/grenfell-tower-mental-health-response-largest-of-its-kind-in-europe. "Dr Green, clinical director at the Grenfell Tower NHS Mental Health Response, said: 'I think this is the biggest programme there's ever been in Europe, certainly in terms of mental health. There's never been anything like it.'" Laura Donnelly, '11,000 people likely to be left suffering PTSD and mental health problems in wake of Grenfell', The Telegraph, 30 October 2017, https://www.telegraph.co.uk/news/2017/10/30/11000-people-likely-left-suffering-ptsd-mental-health-problems/

[37] Interview #26

[38] Interview #24

[39] Interview #13

[40] Interview #19

[41] Interview #10

[42] "Operational (Bronze), Tactical (Silver) and Strategic (Gold) are tiers of command used by each emergency service (and some other organisations). By using this universal structure, the emergency services and other responders will be able to communicate with each other and understand each other's functions and authority. ... A Strategic Commander for each organisation is responsible for formulating the strategy for their organisation's role in the incident. The Strategic Commander retains overall command of their resources but delegates tactical decision making to their Tactical Commander." 'Major Incident Procedure Manual' v9.4, LESLP (2015). https://www.met.police.uk/globalassets/downloads/about-the-met/major-incident-procedure-manual-9th-ed.pdf

[43] Interview #4

[44] Interview #12

[45] Interview #22

[46] Interview #25

[47] Interview #15

[48] C.f. interview #26

[49] Interview #25

[50] Interview #25

[51] Interview #15

Conclusion

This report set out to explore *what* and *how* faith groups responded to Grenfell fire. Our interviewees told us of the faith groups' immediate response: the speed with which they opened the doors to their faith centres, the practical response of sorting and distributing donations, as well as longer-term pastoral, spiritual, and mental health support. Our interviewees also told us how they thought this response had been possible: through the trust the local community had in its faith groups, through the practicalities of the available space the faith centres had, and the faith groups' ability to respond using established protocols as well as spontaneous flexibility in during the crisis.

We also asked our interviewees what lessons they would want Grenfell to offer. Whilst acknowledging that any comparable crisis would always be traumatic and stressful, and impossible ever to prepare for fully, our interviewees emphasised the importance of community cohesion as enabling the best possible response. To this end, we heard of the necessity of faith groups practising their responses, being prepared to use their available networks of staff, volunteers, and neighbours to the best of their ability, as well as developing new friendships with other local faith and voluntary groups.

Our interviewees thought it vital that faith groups be included in and aware of any local authority contingency planning, as well as making themselves known to the local authority being as able and willing to help in need. We heard of the importance of visibility through uniforms or identity markers, both to make oneself available to help, and as a sign of solidarity with the community in crisis.

Lastly, our interviewees emphasised the significance of faith groups being flexible – of being prepared to accept offers of help from those able to give it, and to be able to offer person-centred and religiously sensitive pastoral care, especially to people outside their usual faith group. We also heard how financial donations, rather than physical, can be most helpful in funding the long-term response, and in ensuring there is no 'full-stop' to the support a faith group can offer its community.

There are no glib 'silver linings' to a crisis such as Grenfell. Our interviewees, without exception, expressed how deeply traumatic was the fire, and how, in human terms, nothing could truly make up for it. However, our interviewees also saw some small but significant signs of hope. One was the hope that Grenfell could start a wider conversation about the role of faith communities in Britain today, what they can bring to society, and who should take the lead in responding to a crisis. Another was that the fire would shine a light on housing issues in cities, especially London, and contribute to real change in the availability and standard of housing. In the words of one interviewee:

It was the most horrific time. But the role of the volunteers and the people who came to help and support, showed me God's grace amid the horror. And our ongoing work gives me hope that, whilst nothing can ever make it okay, from great trauma, we might one day find great healing.[1]

[1] Interview #13

Appendices

1a List of interviewees

A large number of individuals and organisations generously gave their time to talk to us about their experiences concerning Grenfell, and this report would, of course, have been impossible without them. There follows a list of interviewees. Please note this list is in alphabetical order and does not correspond with the interview numbers as they occur in the main body of the report. A number of interviewees asked for their names to be withheld from this list: their involvement is acknowledged at the end.

Gurpreet Singh Anand	Central Gurdwara (Khalsa Jatha), London, Managing Trustee
Anja Batista Sonken	The Clement James Centre, Volunteer
Cllr. Mohammed Bakhtiar	RBKC Councillor, St. Helen's Ward
Lotifa Begum	Muslim Aid, Advocacy Co-ordinator
Jackie Blanchflower	Latymer Community Church, Church Leader
Adrian Clee	Regional Community Specialist (Newport Service Centre); National Emergency Response Lead
John Coleby	Caritas, Diocese of Westminster, Director
Sandra Crane	St. Peter's Notting Hill, Church Warden
Revd. Steve Divall	St. Helen's, North Kensington, Vicar
Helen Doery	St. Peter's, Notting Hill, Licensed Lay Minister
Revd. Dr Sean Doherty	St Francis, Dalgarno Way; local resident
Ismahan Egal	Al Manaar Lead Art Therapy Coordinator
Revd. Prebendary Dr Alan Everett	St. Clement and St. James, Priest
Mary-Bridget Flynn-Samuels	Ascension Trust, Development Officer
Captain Karl Gray	Corps Officer, The Salvation Army Clapton Corps, and emergency responder with London Fire Brigade
Captain Ruth Gray	Corps Officer, The Salvation Army Clapton Corps, and emergency responder with London Fire Brigade
Revd. Tom Jackson	Holy Trinity Brompton, Curate; Resurgo, Chief Executive
Revd. Mike Long	Notting Hill Methodist Church, Minister
Sailesh Mehta	St. Peter's Notting Hill, Treasurer
Abu Mumin	Eden Care, Social Worker
Revd. Mark O'Donoghue	Christ Church Kensington, Vicar, & Area Dean
Lydia Rye	Citizens UK, Senior Organiser, West London Citizens
Abdurahman Sayed	Al Manaar Muslim Cultural Heritage Centre, CEO
Nic Schlagman	West London Synagogue, Head of Social Action and Interfaith

Major Paul Scott	Corps Officer, The Salvation Army Notting Hill Corps
Father Gerard Skinner	St. Francis of Assisi, Notting Hill, Priest
Revd. Robert Thompson	St. Clement and St. James, Self Stipendary Minister; RBKC Councillor, Dalgarno Ward; Chair of the Grenfell Scrutiny Committee
The Rt Revd Dr Graham Tomlin	Bishop of Kensington
Cllr. Mary Weale	RBKC Councillor, Brompton and Hans Town Ward, Lead Member for Communities
Yvette Williams MBE	Justice 4 Grenfell, Campaign Co-ordinator
Pastor Derrick Wilson	Tabernacle Christian Centre, Senior Pastor

Plus three interviewees who chose to remain anonymous.

1b Interviewing survivors

We were very keen to ensure that survivors' voices were heard in our research, and that our findings reflected their experiences of the fire and its aftermath. However, we were acutely aware of the sensitivities involved in contacting survivors and the bereaved, and in no way wished to intrude on their grief and process of healing. To this end, we asked some of our community contacts who were appropriately placed to do so to consider speaking to some survivors and others in the community on our behalf.

This was on the explicit understanding that those approached would be aware their answers would be relayed to us and included in our research, and subject to the same confidentiality and ethics guidelines as our regular interviews. We asked the participants approaching survivors on our behalf to speak to as wide a range of individuals willing to contribute as possible, and offered them a brief list of example questions – with the caveat that they were free to adapt or amend the questions as appropriate.

These questions were:

— Tell us about your experience of faith groups you encountered at the time of the tragedy or afterwards. Whom did you encounter?

— What did they do – at the time of the crisis, in the following weeks, since then?

— What did you think about their help? Was there anything that made a real difference? Was there anything that was a problem, or which could have been done better?

— Do you have any other comments and reflections?

As with our regular interviewees, these survivors and other members of the local community were free to choose either to be named in the list of participants, or to remain anonymous.

2 Ethics guidelines

Theos provided all interviewees and interested parties with ethics and confidentiality guidelines, which were presented to each potential interviewee for their approval before their respective interviews took place. Due to the sensitivities around this project, we enhanced our usual guidelines to afford additional protection and flexibility for participants, and also were able to tailor the guidelines to suit individual participants' requirements, if needed.

Our ethics guidelines were as follows:

— Interviews will be conducted by a Theos researcher, in private, at a location of the interviewee's choice;

— All interviews will have the written consent of interviewee;

- All interviews will follow planned guidelines to lead the conversation, but will also be shaped by the particular experiences and views of the interviewee. Interviewees are free to decline to answer any question for any reason, and to withdraw from the interview process at any time;

- All interviews will be audio (but not video) recorded, and recordings will be held on a password-protected drive, available only to the Theos team working on the project;

- Interviews will not be transcribed but may be quoted in the final report. All identifying references to interviewees will be removed and all quotations will be anonymously ascribed, e.g. "Interview #4";

- Interviewees are welcome to bring a chaperone or support person, if they wish, who would be expected to keep to the same levels of confidentiality;

- Interviewees will be shown their quotations in advance of any publication, and are free to withdraw their contribution at any time during the interview process. Anyone quoted in the report will be given the opportunity to check their words in advance, and a draft copy of the report can be made available to those interviewees who wish to read it.

3 Interview questions

As noted in Appendix 2, flexibility was built into each of the interviews to reflect and respect particular experiences. What follows here, therefore, are the questions that formed the baseline of the interviews, rather than the exact questions asked in each.

1. Could you tell us a bit about yourself? Occupation, the length of time you've lived in or around Grenfell Tower and the Lancaster West Estate, your involvement in your local faith group, etc.?

   If we had contacted you this time last year about a different project, and asked you about your general experience of the area, your perceptions of the community, faith groups, and the local council before 14 June 2017, what would you have said?

2. *Crisis*: 24-72 hours.

   Where were you on evening of 13 June? What was the first you heard?

   If appropriate – could you tell us what unfolded as you saw it? What was your role, if any? What did you do?

   What was your perception and experience of the initial emergency response?

   Who did you speak to/ see act during the immediate crisis? Which faith groups were most evident and what were they doing? How did you know the faith groups were present and working (food banks, clothes, offering rooms, etc.) – who told you?

   Who was meeting the immediate practical needs of accommodation, food, and clothing?

3. *Medium term:* 72 hrs-1 month.

   What has been your perception and experience of the medium term response? E.g., what has been done by faith groups in campaigning and ongoing practical, emotional, and spiritual support? How has this been received?

Were faith groups trusted, and seen as more communicative than the Council? Why/why not?

What has/ has not worked?

What new relationships/ networks were forged or enabled?

4   *Long term:* 1 month-ongoing.

What has been your perception and experience of the long term response?

In light of what we've discussed, what most impressed you with the faith groups' response? What worked best?

What can we learn from it, or do again, either in a crisis or in peacetime?

Plus the reverse – what problems were there? What needs went unmet?

Were faith groups any more able to respond than either the non-religious community groups or statutory authorities?

How have faith groups been offering/meeting ongoing needs? (E.g., counselling, legal or financial aid, six month memorial service at St Paul's Cathedral.)

What was your perception of the six month memorial service at St Paul's?

What new relationships have developed and lasted? How has Grenfell changed the style of those relationships?

How has it changed the community? How have the local faith communities adapted or changed? What effect has that had on the broader West London community?

How has it changed or confirmed your opinion of local faith groups, including your own?

What has enabled or barred faith groups' response and action?

If appropriate – how has this experience affected your faith?

5. Are there any other groups you believe we should speak to?

Theos – enriching conversations

Theos exists to enrich the conversation about the role of faith in society.

Religion and faith have become key public issues in this century, nationally and globally. As our society grows more religiously diverse, we must grapple with religion as a significant force in public life. All too often, though, opinions in this area are reactionary or ill informed.

We exist to change this

We want to help people move beyond common misconceptions about faith and religion, behind the headlines and beneath the surface. Our rigorous approach gives us the ability to express informed views with confidence and clarity.

As the UK's leading religion and society think tank, we reach millions of people with our ideas. Through our reports, events and media commentary, we influence today's influencers and decision makers. According to *The Economist*, we're "an organisation that demands attention." We believe Christianity can contribute to the common good and that faith, given space in the public square, will help the UK to flourish.

Will you partner with us?

Theos receives no government, corporate or denominational funding. We rely on donations from individuals and organisations to continue our vital work. Please consider signing up as a Theos Friend or Associate or making a one off donation today.

Theos Friends and Students
- Stay up to date with our monthly newsletter
- Receive (free) printed copies of our reports
- Get free tickets to all our events

£75 / year for Friends £40 / year for Students

Theos Associates
- Stay up to date with our monthly newsletter
- Receive (free) printed copies of our reports
- Get free tickets to all our events
- Get invites to private events with the Theos team and other Theos Associates

£375 / year

Sign up on our website:
www.theosthinktank.co.uk/about/support-us